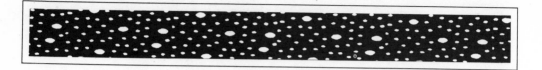

WILD ABOUT POTATOES

BY MARIE BIANCO

D1400799

BARRON'S

Woodbury, New York • London • Toronto • Sydney

For Frank, Bill, Mary, Jim, Sue, and, especially, Michael.

All inquiries should be addressed to:
Barron's Educational Series, Inc.
113 Crossways Park Drive
Woodbury, New York 11797

Library of Congress No. 85-1392
International Standard Book No. 0-8120-2914-3

Library of Congress Cataloging in Publication Data
Bianco, Marie.
   Wild about potatoes.

   Includes index.
   1. Cookery (Potatoes)   I. Title.
TX803.P8B53   1985   641.6′521   85-1392
ISBN 0-8120-2914-3

Design by Milton Glaser Inc.
Color photographs by Karen Leeds
Helga Weinrib, food stylist
Linda Peacock, prop stylist

Photo 1 opposite page 16: cream and blue platter
courtesy of Dean & DeLuca.

PRINTED IN THE UNITED STATES OF AMERICA

5 6 7 8 9   510   9 8 7 6 5 4 3 2

CONTENTS

INTRODUCTION
5

CONVERSION TABLES
6

ABOUT POTATOES
8

POTATO BASICS
*Potato favorites, from french fries and chips
to potato pancakes and hash browns*
13

POTATO SOUPS AND SALADS
*Hearty soups and hot or cold salads,
all on a potato theme*
23

POTATOES UNLIMITED
*Potatoes combined with other vegetables
for new taste combinations,
and potatoes meant to accompany main dishes*
33

ETHNIC POTATOES
Potato dishes from around the world
47

POTATO MAIN DISHES
Substantial meals centered on the potato
59

POTATO SNACKS

Potato skins, with dips and toppings,
and baked potatoes with a myriad of stuffings

69

POTATO CREPES

A new taste for an elegant dish

79

POTATO BAKED GOODS

Some baking you can do with potatoes
lending the flavor and moisture

83

POTATO DESSERTS

Surprising sweets made with potatoes

87

INDEX
90

INTRODUCTION

P otato dishes—like bread and pasta—become a way of life, and cooks rarely change their recipes. Oh, they'll try some new food like arugula or attempt a different kind of cooking, like Chinese, but the basics are basic, and that they remain.

I remember an afternoon when one of my sons came home after having had dinner at his friend's home. He said his friend's mother made the best potatoes he ever had. Because I didn't think this kid's mother was all that terrific a cook, I questioned him about what made those potatoes so good. "The mashed potatoes had lumps in them," he said.

Well, my mashed potatoes didn't have lumps. At least up until that time. But if this kid wanted lumps, lumps he would get. (Of course, I rationalized that my potatoes were whipped, not mashed.) But I realized that there might be a better way—and I learned from that. There is no one way to make a dish, and if a kid wants lumps, give him lumps.

And so, this book gives the basics. But it also gives recipes that are a little different from the "tried and true." By the way, I think the recipe for the chocolate potato cake is my favorite. The potatoes give the cake a moist, chewy texture that blends with the chocolate flavor very well. No one had to be urged to have seconds on that cake.

CONVERSION TABLES

The weights and measures in the lists of ingredients and cooking instructions for each recipe are in both U.S. and metric units.

LIQUID MEASURES

The Imperial cup is considerably larger than the U.S. cup. Use the following table to convert to Imperial liquid units.

AMERICAN CUP (in book)	IMPERIAL CUP (adjusts to)
¼ cup	4 tablespoons
⅓ cup	5 tablespoons
½ cup	8 tablespoons
⅔ cup	¼ pint
¾ cup	¼ pint + 2 tablespoons
1 cup	¼ pint + 6 tablespoons
1¼ cups	½ pint
1½ cups	½ pint + 4 tablespoons
2 cups	¾ pint
2½ cups	1 pint
3 cups	1½ pints
4 cups	1½ pints + 4 tablespoons
5 cups	2 pints

Note: The Australian and Canadian cup measures 250 mL and is only slightly larger than the U.S. cup, which is 236 mL. Cooks in Australia and Canada can follow the exact measurements given in the recipes, using either the U.S. or metric measures.

SOLID MEASURES

British and Australian cooks measure more items by weight. Here are approximate equivalents for basic items.

	U.S. Customary	Imperial
Butter	1 tablespoon	½ oz.
	¼ cup	2 oz.
	½ cup	4 oz.
	1 cup	8 oz.
Cheese (grated)	½ cup	2 oz.
Flour (sifted)	¼ cup	1¼ oz.
	½ cup	2½ oz.
	1 cup	5 oz.
	1½ cups	7½ oz.
	2 cups	10 oz.
Herbs (fresh, chopped)	¼ cup	¼ oz.
Vegetables, chopped	½ cup	2 oz.
	1 cup	4 oz.

OVEN TEMPERATURES

British cooks should use the following settings.

Gas Mark	¼	2	4	6	8
Fahrenheit	225	300	350	400	450
Celsius	110	150	175	200	230

ABOUT POTATOES

Potatoes have a lot going for them. In spite of their rather unattractive brown and bumpy appearance, they are the world's favorite vegetable. People consume more potatoes in more ways than any other vegetable available today. Potatoes are basic. They can be eaten alone, or in combination with other vegetables or with meat. Potatoes also add a moist and chewy quality to bread and baked goods.

Potatoes come in four basic varieties: russet, long white, round white, and round red.

Russet potatoes are brown and rough with a scaly and netted skin and are best for baking or when you want potatoes to keep their shape when fried or sautéed. Should you choose to mash them in a food processor, they tend to become gluey.

The Russet Burbank was developed by Luther Burbank and this potato is chiefly grown in Idaho.

Long whites are light buff in color, thin-skinned, and waxy. They are good for frying and make perfect potato salad because they do not break apart when boiled.

Round whites are brown or buff in color, round or elliptical in shape, and are best used for mashing or for baking when you want a mealy potato.

Round reds are red-skinned and are good for boiling or in potato salads.

"New" potatoes are not a variety of potato at all but rather small, immature potatoes with a papery skin that come to market directly from harvesting, and skip storage altogether.

Although some varieties of potatoes are labeled "all purpose" many cooks prefer one potato over another. By experimenting with a variety of types you will come up with your own favorites for various cooking methods. After all, we use different types of apples, tomatoes, even parsley. Why be limited to one type of potato?

Since so many of the nutrients in potatoes are stored directly below the skin, whenever possible leave the skins on rather than peel them.

The fruitful potato is ready for harvest in 90 to 120 days and gets high marks for nutrition. One medium potato contains only 100 calories and is virtually free of both fat and salt. Boiled in its skin, the potato contains 2.1 grams protein, 22 grams carbohydrates, 6 milligrams iron, 90 milligrams thiamine, 40 milligrams riboflavin, 1.5 milligrams niacin, 16 milligrams vitamin C, plus magnesium, phosphorus, calcium, and copper.

Potatoes do not store well at home. They like a cool, but not cold, dry place. Kept in the refrigerator, the starch will turn to sugar and the potatoes will have a sweet taste when cooked. The potatoes will also darken in color.

During the fall when they are being harvested, potatoes are available at bargain prices, but if you store them improperly, they will eventually sprout eyes and become spongy and have to be discarded. If the eyes are not too large, break them off and use the potatoes immediately. Never wash potatoes before storing since this hastens decay.

Do not purchase potatoes with patches of green skin, if possible. This change in skin color occurs when immature potatoes have been exposed to light. If eaten, this portion of the potato can cause discomfort. Instead, cut off and discard any green portions before cooking.

Once the staff of life for peasants of the world, the versatile potato is the delight of just about every cuisine— about 130 different countries grow potatoes worth over 1 billion dollars at the consumer level. The hardy potato will grow at sea level as well as in mountains, deserts, and northern regions.

Besides being used as food, the plentiful potato is also fed to livestock, distilled into vodka and aquavit, and used as starch, paste, and dye. Experiments are being conducted to turn potatoes into ethyl alcohol to fuel cars. Now you can eat your potato and drive it too.

The potato is a relative of the deadly nightshade family, and when first introduced to Europe, it was condemned as evil and many believed its consumption led to disease. First cultivated by the Inca Indians in Peru over two thousand years ago, potatoes were introduced to Europe by the Spanish explorers. A French pharmacist Antoine Parmentier is responsible for increasing its popularity. He became acquainted with potatoes during the Seven Years War when he was a German prisoner. He wined and dined the nobility of Europe with all-potato dinners in his home. One of his guests at a twenty-potato dish reception was none other than Benjamin Franklin. Later Franklin introduced the potato to Thomas Jefferson, who grew the plant in his garden at Monticello. To this day, whenever you see the word Parmentier in the name of a recipe, you can be sure it contains potatoes.

Potatoes are nourishing, healthy, versatile, inexpensive. And they taste good. What better reasons for eating "pommes de terre," the apples of the earth?

POTATO BASICS

FRENCH-FRIED POTATOES

SERVES 4 TO 6

6 russet potatoes
vegetable oil
salt

Wash potatoes and peel, if desired. Slice lengthwise into ¼-inch (¾-cm) slices. Stack slices and cut lengthwise into ¼-inch (¾-cm) fingers. Soak in cold water for 20 minutes. Remove and wipe dry.

In a 9- or 10-inch (23- or 25-cm) skillet, heat the oil to 350°F (180°C) and cook potatoes, a few at a time, for 4 to 5 minutes. Remove and drain on paper towel.

Just before serving, reheat oil to 390°F (200°C) and fry potatoes a second time until they are crisp and golden brown. Drain well on paper towels and sprinkle with salt.

Wash potatoes and peel, if desired. Slice potatoes as thin as possible using a sharp knife or a food processor. Soak potatoes for 15 minutes in cold water. Drain and wipe dry.

In a 9- or 10-inch (23- or 25-cm) skillet, heat oil to 360°F (180°C) and fry slices a few at a time. Drain well on paper towels and sprinkle with salt.

POTATO CHIPS

SERVES 4 TO 6

6 russet potatoes
vegetable oil
salt

HASH BROWN POTATOES

SERVES 8

10 cups (1 kg) coarsely chopped
cooked potatoes (either baked
or boiled)
salt and pepper to taste
1 small onion, minced
½ pound (225 g) sliced bacon

Season potatoes with salt and pepper. Stir in onion, blending well.

In a large, heavy skillet, cook bacon until crisp. Drain bacon, reserving drippings in pan. Crumble bacon and set aside.

Add the potatoes to skillet and cook, stirring occasionally, until they are golden brown, about 15 minutes. Add bacon pieces and serve.

Or cook potatoes and bacon pieces without turning until a crisp brown crust forms on the bottom. Invert onto a serving platter and serve immediately.

Opposite: Hash Brown Potatoes

Wash potatoes and pat dry. Cut into wedges and toss with olive oil.

In a small bowl, combine oregano, chives, salt, pepper, Parmesan cheese, and bread crumbs. Dip the potato wedges in the mixture and place skin side down in a shallow baking pan.

Bake for about 30 minutes, or until potatoes are tender.

OVEN-FRIED POTATO WEDGES

SERVES 4

Preheat oven to 425°F (215°C)

4 russet potatoes
½ cup (125 mL) olive oil
1 tablespoon finely chopped fresh oregano, or 1 teaspoon dried
1 tablespoon finely chopped fresh chives, or 1 teaspoon dried
1 teaspoon salt
½ teaspoon pepper
2 tablespoons grated Parmesan cheese
2 tablespoons unseasoned bread crumbs

FRIED POTATOES AND ONIONS

SERVES 6

6 potatoes
2 onions
¼ cup (60 g) butter
¼ cup (60 mL) vegetable oil
salt and pepper

Scrub potatoes and slice ⅛ inch (½ cm) thick. Peel onions and slice ⅛ inch (½ cm) thick.

In a large, heavy skillet, melt butter and add oil. Add onions and cook for 3 minutes or until tender. Add half the potato slices and stir-fry for 2 minutes. Add remaining potatoes and cook, stirring frequently, until they become brown on bottom. Turn potatoes with spatula and bring browned portion to the top. Brown on second side and cook until tender. Invert onto serving plate. Sprinkle with salt and pepper. Serve immediately.

With a sharp paring knife, cut a ½-inch (1½-cm)-wide band around the middle of each potato, discarding skin. Wash potatoes and place in a large saucepan with boiling salted water to cover. Cook for 20 minutes or until tender; drain.

In the same saucepan melt butter and stir in salt, pepper, and parsley. Return potatoes to pan and shake to coat potatoes with butter. Transfer to serving dish and serve immediately.

NEW POTATOES WITH PARSLEY AND BUTTER

SERVES 6

2 pounds (900 g) new potatoes, either red or white
6 tablespoons (85 g) unsalted butter
salt and pepper to taste
¼ cup (7 g) chopped fresh Italian parsley

ROASTED POTATOES

SERVES 6

Preheat oven to 325°F (160°C)

6 potatoes
vegetable oil, as needed
3 onions, sliced
4- to 6-pound (1¾- to 2¾-kg) beef,
lamb, or pork roast

Peel potatoes and cut into large chunks. If roast is very lean, roll potatoes in vegetable oil. Place meat in baking pan and roast as you prefer.

About 1½ hours before meat is cooked, add potatoes and onions to pan. Stir with spoon to cover them with pan juices. Cook until meat is tender and potatoes are done.

In a small bowl, mix together raw potatoes, flour, onion, egg, salt, and pepper.

In a large, heavy skillet, pour in enough oil to coat bottom. Heat oil over medium heat. Pour in scant ¼ cupful (60 mL) of potato mixture, 3 or 4 at a time, and flatten into circles with the back of a spoon.

Fry for 3 minutes or until browned and crisp; turn and brown other side. Add additional oil as necessary. Drain on paper towels. If thinner pancakes are desired, add 1 to 2 tablespoons vegetable oil to batter.

POTATO PANCAKES

MAKES ABOUT 12 PANCAKES

2½ cups (285 g) coarsely shredded
raw potatoes
½ cup (70 g) all-purpose flour
1 small onion, grated
1 egg
salt and pepper to taste
vegetable oil

MASHED POTATOES

SERVES 4

4 large potatoes
1 cup (240 mL) milk or cream
¼ cup (60 g) butter
salt and pepper to taste

Pare potatoes and cut into quarters, roughly the same size. Place in a large saucepan with 1 inch (2½ cm) of cold water. Bring to a boil, cover, lower heat, and cook for about 25 to 30 minutes, or until tender. Drain well in colander.

Place potatoes in mixing bowl of electric mixer and beat until smooth.

Heat milk or cream in small saucepan and add to potatoes along with butter, salt, and pepper. Beat until smooth and fluffy.

POTATO SOUPS AND SALADS

POLISH POTATO AND SAUSAGE SOUP

SERVES 6

2 tablespoons (30 g) butter
1 pound (450 g) kielbasa, sliced
1 large onion, chopped
4 stalks celery, chopped
4 cups (340 g) shredded cabbage
2 cups (225 g) diced carrots
1 bay leaf
1 tablespoon finely chopped fresh
thyme, or 1 teaspoon dried
2 tablespoons wine vinegar
1 teaspoon salt
3 cups (700 mL) beef bouillon
3 cups (700 mL) water
4 potatoes, peeled and cubed

In a large stockpot, melt butter and sauté kielbasa, onion, and celery until vegetables are tender. Add cabbage, carrots, bay leaf, thyme, vinegar, salt, beef bouillon, and water.

Cover and simmer for 1 hour. Add potatoes, cover, and cook 20 minutes longer or until potatoes are tender. Remove bay leaf and serve.

Opposite: Mashed Potatoes (p. 22)

Place potatoes in a medium saucepan, cover with water, and cook, covered, for 20 minutes or until tender. Drain well.

In a medium skillet, cook bacon until crisp. Remove bacon, reserving drippings. Drain bacon and crumble.

In a large saucepan, cook onion in bacon drippings for 5 minutes or until tender. Add salt, white pepper, nutmeg, mustard, and Worcestershire sauce.

Mash potatoes and blend in half-and-half. Add to onion mixture and cook until heated through, but do not boil. Add parsley, shredded Swiss cheese, and crumbled bacon. Heat, but do not boil.

CREAM OF POTATO SOUP

SERVES 4 TO 6

2 pounds (900 g) potatoes, peeled and cut into quarters
6 slices bacon, chopped
1 onion, chopped
1 teaspoon salt
½ teaspoon white pepper
½ teaspoon grated nutmeg
¼ teaspoon dry mustard
1 teaspoon Worcestershire sauce
3 cups (700 mL) half-and-half
2 tablespoons chopped fresh Italian parsley
1 cup (115 g) shredded Swiss cheese

MUSSEL POTATO CHOWDER

SERVES 4

1 pound firm fresh fish
2 tablespoons (30 g) butter
1 onion, chopped
1 carrot, pared and diced
2 cups (225 g) diced raw potatoes
1 bottle (8 ounces/225 g) clam juice
2 cups (425 mL) water
1 small bay leaf
1½ teaspoons finely chopped fresh thyme, or ½ teaspoon dried
salt and pepper to taste
2 dozen mussels, steamed and removed from shell

Cut fish into 1-inch (2½-cm) cubes.

In a stockpot, melt butter and sauté onion, carrot, and potatoes. Add fish, clam juice, water, bay leaf, thyme, salt, and pepper. Cook about 20 minutes or until vegetables are tender. Remove bay leaf.

Add mussels and heat through, but do not boil.

In a large saucepan, combine 1 cup (115 g) potatoes, chicken stock, onion, and salt. Cover and cook over medium heat for 10 to 15 minutes or until potatoes are tender. Add sage, paprika, and pepper. Pour mixture into the container of an electric blender or food processor and puree.

Return mixture to saucepan and add remaining 1½ cups (170 g) potatoes, carrots, peas, corn, celery, and milk. Lower heat; cover; simmer for 15 minutes or until potatoes are tender. Add cooked turkey and heat 5 minutes longer.

TURKEY POTATO CHOWDER

SERVES 6

2½ cups (285 g) diced peeled potato
2½ cups (225 g) chicken stock
1 small onion, chopped
½ teaspoon salt
1½ teaspoons finely chopped fresh sage, or ½ teaspoon dried
¼ teaspoon paprika
⅛ teaspoon pepper
½ cup (60 g) thinly sliced carrots
½ cup (60 g) green peas, fresh or frozen
½ cup (60 g) corn niblets
½ cup (60 g) sliced celery
3 cups (700 mL) milk
1 cup (175 g) diced cooked turkey

BEEF AND POTATO SOUP, HUNGARIAN STYLE

SERVES 4 TO 6

¼ cup (60 g) butter
1 pound (240 g) lean beef chuck,
cut into ½-inch (1½-cm) cubes
2 medium onions, coarsely chopped
¼ cup (35 g) all-purpose flour
2 tablespoons Hungarian paprika
2 cups (225 g) chopped peeled
fresh tomatoes
1 tablespoon finely chopped fresh
marjoram, or 1 teaspoon dried
2 tablespoons chopped fresh parsley
2 cans (10½ ounces/300 g each)
condensed beef broth
2 cups (425 mL) water
½ teaspoon salt
2 cups (225 g) cubed peeled potatoes
2 carrots, pared and diced
sour cream for garnish

In a large saucepan, melt butter and add beef and onion. Cook for 10 minutes or until beef is browned and onion is tender. Sprinkle with flour and paprika, and mix well. Add tomatoes, marjoram, parsley, beef broth, water, and salt. Bring to a boil, lower heat, cover, and simmer, stirring occasionally, for 45 minutes.

Add potatoes and carrots; cover; cook 20 minutes longer or until vegetables are tender. Ladle into bowls and garnish with a dollop of sour cream.

Cook potatoes in lightly salted water for 20 minutes or until tender. Drain and cool slightly. Peel and cut into ¼-inch (¾-cm) slices.

In large skillet, melt butter; add shallots and cook, stirring constantly, for 2 minutes taking care not to brown them. Blend in flour, curry powder, and salt. Cook, stirring constantly, for 2 minutes. Slowly stir in chicken broth and vinegar and cook until thickened, stirring constantly.

Add potatoes, apple, celery, raisins, and chicken. Heat thoroughly but do not boil. Sprinkle with almonds. Serve over hot rice.

CURRIED CHICKEN AND POTATO SALAD

SERVES 6

6 medium potatoes
⅓ cup (75 g) butter
2 tablespoons chopped shallots
3 tablespoons all-purpose flour
1 teaspoon curry powder, or to taste
½ teaspoon salt
1¼ cups (300 mL) chicken broth
2 tablespoons cider vinegar
1 Granny Smith apple, pared, cored
and cut into thin slices
½ cup (60 g) sliced celery
2 tablespoons light raisins
2 cups (340 g) cooked diced chicken
½ cup (60 g) slivered almonds
hot cooked rice

29

HOT HAM-AND-EGGS POTATO SALAD

SERVES 6 TO 8

12 small potatoes
3 tablespoons (45 g) butter
½ cup (60 g) chopped onion
2 tablespoons all-purpose flour
1 teaspoon salt
¼ teaspoon pepper
½ cup (125 mL) cider vinegar
½ cup (125 mL) water
1 cup (115 g) sliced celery
1 teaspoon caraway seeds
3 cups (500 g) diced cooked ham
3 hard-cooked eggs,
    coarsely chopped
½ cup (60 g) chopped green pepper
1 carrot, pared and shredded

In a large saucepan, cook potatoes, covered, in lightly salted water for 20 minutes or until tender. Drain and cool slightly. Peel and cut into chunks.

In a large skillet, melt butter. Add onion and cook for 5 minutes, taking care not to brown onion. Stir in flour, salt, and pepper and blend well. Stir in vinegar and water and stir over medium heat until mixture boils.

Add celery, caraway seeds, potatoes, ham, eggs, green pepper, and carrot. Toss lightly. Heat thoroughly but do not boil. Serve immediately.

In a large saucepan, cook potatoes, covered, in boiling salted water for 20 minutes or until tender. Drain; cool slightly, peel, and cut into chunks. Add oil, onion, lemon juice, salt, and pepper; toss lightly and set aside for 1 to 2 hours.

Add celery, green pepper, parsley, scallion, eggs, mustard, and mayonnaise. Mix lightly. Line salad bowl with lettuce and pile salad on top.

CALIFORNIA POTATO SALAD

SERVES 6 TO 8

1½ pounds (680 g) potatoes
2 tablespoons vegetable oil
1 tablespoon chopped fresh onion
1 tablespoon fresh lemon juice
1 teaspoon salt
¼ teaspoon pepper
1 cup (115 g) chopped celery
¼ cup (30 g) chopped green pepper
2 tablespoons chopped fresh parsley
1 scallion, chopped
4 hard-cooked eggs,
  coarsely chopped
1 teaspoon Dijon-style mustard
½ cup (125 mL) mayonnaise
lettuce leaves

POTATO VEGETABLE SALAD

SERVES 6 TO 8

3 medium potatoes, cooked
and peeled
½ cup (125 mL) wine vinegar
¼ cup (60 mL) olive oil
salt and pepper to taste
½ head cauliflower, broken into
flowerettes
2 cups (225 g) broccoli flowerettes
½ pound (225 g) asparagus, cut into
½-inch (1½-cm) pieces
½ cup (60 g) fresh or frozen green
peas, cooked
3 scallions, chopped
1 carrot, pared and shredded
8 cherry tomatoes, halved
romaine lettuce
chopped green pepper, for garnish

Cut hot potatoes into chunks. Place in large bowl. Combine vinegar, oil, salt, and pepper in screw-top jar; shake well. Pour over hot potatoes and toss lightly. Cover and refrigerate.

Steam cauliflower, broccoli, and asparagus separately for 10 minutes or until just crisp-tender. Refrigerate to chill.

Just before serving, combine potatoes, cauliflower, broccoli, asparagus, peas, scallions, carrots, and tomatoes. Toss lightly and serve on romaine lettuce leaves. Garnish with chopped green pepper.

Opposite: Potato Vegetable Salad

POTATOES UNLIMITED

NEW POTATOES AND CARROTS

SERVES 6

1½ pounds (680 g) small new
potatoes
1 cup (240 mL) beef stock
or bouillon
4 carrots, pared, cut on the diagonal
into ¼-inch (¾-cm) slices
¼ cup (60 g) butter, melted
2 tablespoons chopped fresh
Italian parsley
1½ teaspoons finely chopped fresh
tarragon, or ½ teaspoon dried
1 scallion, chopped
salt and pepper to taste

Scrub potatoes; place in a medium saucepan with beef bouillon. Bring to a boil, cover, and steam 10 minutes. Add carrot slices. Cover and steam 5 minutes longer or until vegetables are tender. Drain vegetables, reserving ¼ cup (60 mL) cooking liquid.

Combine liquid with butter, parsley, tarragon, scallion, salt, and pepper. Toss lightly with vegetables.

Cook rutabaga and potatoes separately, covered, in lightly salted water for 20 minutes or until tender.

In a small saucepan, melt butter and cook onion for 5 minutes or until tender. When potatoes and rutabaga are done, drain them and place in large bowl of electric mixer.

Beat mixture until smooth. Add onion and parsley, cream, salt, pepper, and nutmeg. Mix well. Add additional cream if mixture is too thick.

MASHED POTATOES AND RUTABAGAS

SERVES 6

2 cups (225 g) cubed raw rutabaga
2 cups (225 g) cubed raw potatoes
salt
2 tablespoons (30 g) butter
1 small onion, chopped
2 tablespoons chopped fresh
Italian parsley
2 tablespoons light cream
½ teaspoon salt
¼ teaspoon pepper
¼ teaspoon grated nutmeg

POTATO AND SPINACH CASSEROLE

SERVES 8

Preheat oven to 350°F (180°C)

2 packages (10 ounces/285 g each) frozen chopped spinach, defrosted; or 2 pounds (900 g) fresh spinach, cooked, drained and chopped

6 medium potatoes

3 eggs

¼ cup (60 g) butter, melted

1 teaspoon salt

¼ teaspoon pepper

2 tablespoons chopped onion

2 tablespoons chopped fresh Italian parsley

1 tablespoon finely chopped fresh dill, or ½ teaspoon dill weed

8 ounces (225 g) feta cheese, crumbled

½ cup (60 g) grated Parmesan cheese

2 tablespoons (30 g) butter

Squeeze as much water as possible from spinach. Set spinach aside.

Peel and shred potatoes. Mix potatoes with eggs, melted butter, salt, pepper, onion, parsley, and dill. Turn half of mixture into a buttered shallow 2-quart (2-L) casserole. Cover with all the spinach and feta. Top with remaining potato mixture. Cover and bake for 30 minutes. Remove cover, sprinkle with Parmesan cheese, and dot with 2 tablespoons (30 g) butter. Bake 30 minutes longer.

In a medium bowl, mash potatoes and add milk. Cut peppers in half, removing seeds and membranes. Parboil in salted water in large saucepan for 10 minutes. Drain.

To mashed potatoes in the bowl, add carrots, mushrooms, parsley, scallions, cheddar cheese, salt, pepper, and thyme. Mix well. Pile mixture into drained green pepper halves. Bake in oven for 12 minutes.

POTATO-STUFFED PEPPERS

SERVES 6

Preheat oven to 425°F (215°C)

1½ pounds (680 g) potatoes, cooked and peeled

¾ cup (175 mL) milk

3 medium green peppers

1 cup (115 g) peeled and shredded carrots

½ cup (60 g) chopped mushrooms

2 tablespoons chopped fresh parsley

2 tablespoons sliced scallions

½ cup (60 g) shredded cheddar cheese

salt and pepper to taste

1½ teaspoons finely chopped fresh thyme, or ½ teaspoon dried

POTATOES WITH GREEN BEANS AND RED ONIONS

SERVES 6

2 cups (225 g) cold cooked fresh
green beans, cut in 1-inch
(2½-cm) pieces

2 cups (225 g) diced cold
cooked potatoes

2 cups (225 g) chopped celery

1 large red onion, cut in rings

6 tablespoons (85 mL) olive oil

2 tablespoons red wine vinegar

salt and pepper to taste

½ teaspoon finely chopped fresh
oregano, or ⅛ teaspoon dried

In a large bowl, combine green beans, potatoes, celery, and onion.

In a jar with a tight-fitting lid, combine olive oil, wine vinegar, salt, pepper, and oregano. Shake well. Pour over vegetables. Chill for about 30 minutes before serving.

Shred potato and zucchini using large-hole side of a 4-sided grater or food processor. (There should be 1 cup (115 g) of shredded potato and 2 cups (225 g) of shredded zucchini.) Place vegetables in a large bowl. Add onion, cornmeal, parsley, salt, pepper, Parmesan cheese, and eggs and stir well.

In a large skillet, heat 1 tablespoon each butter and olive oil. Drop potato mixture by heaping tablespoonfuls into skillet. Fry for 3 minutes or until golden brown on bottom; turn and brown second side. Add remaining butter and oil as needed.

POTATO-ZUCCHINI FRITTERS

MAKES ABOUT 12 FRITTERS

1 large potato, peeled
2 medium zucchini
¼ cup (30 g) chopped onion
¼ cup (40 g) cornmeal
2 tablespoons chopped fresh
Italian parsley
1 teaspoon salt
½ teaspoon pepper
2 tablespoons grated
Parmesan cheese
3 eggs, slightly beaten
2 tablespoons (30 g) butter
2 tablespoons olive oil

POTATO FRITTERS

SERVES 8

1 cup (240 mL) water
¼ cup (60 g) unsalted butter
½ teaspoon salt
1 cup (140 g) all-purpose flour
4 eggs
4 medium potatoes
freshly ground black pepper
vegetable oil for deep-frying

In a medium saucepan, heat water, butter, and salt until water comes to a full boil. Add flour all at once and stir with a wooden spoon until it forms a ball and leaves the side of the pan. Remove pan from heat and add eggs, one at a time, beating well after each addition.

Peel potatoes and cook in lightly salted water in large covered saucepan for 20 minutes or until tender. Drain, cool slightly and place through ricer or food mill. Add salt, if necessary, and season with pepper. Beat potatoes into flour/egg mixture.

Heat oil to depth of 2 inches (5 cm) in large skillet, preferably an electric fry pan, to 360°F (180°C). Drop mixture by tablespoonfuls into hot fat and fry 5 minutes or until golden, turning once. (Fritters will puff up as they cook.) Drain on paper towels and serve immediately.

Opposite: Potato Fritters

Peel potatoes and cook, covered, in lightly salted water in large saucepan for 20 minutes or until tender. Drain and mash. Remove casing from Italian sausage.

In large skillet, heat olive oil, add sausage meat, and sauté 10 minutes or until it loses its pink color. Add mushrooms and celery and sauté for 3 minutes. Drain well and add to mashed potatoes along with salt, pepper, sage, parsley, and egg. Mix well.

POTATO STUFFING FOR TURKEY

MAKES ENOUGH STUFFING FOR A 10-POUND (4½-kg) TURKEY

4 medium potatoes
½ pound (225 g) Italian sausage
2 tablespoons olive oil
1 cup (115 g) chopped mushrooms
½ cup (60 g) chopped celery
salt and pepper to taste
1½ teaspoons finely chopped fresh sage, or ½ teaspoon dried
1 tablespoon chopped fresh parsley
1 egg

TWICE-BAKED POTATOES

SERVES 6

Preheat oven to 400°F (200°C)

6 large russet potatoes
1 cup (240 mL) half-and-half, warmed
¼ cup (60 g) butter, cut in pats
4 ounces cheddar cheese, shredded
4 slices bacon, cooked and crumbled
1 teaspoon salt
½ teaspoon freshly ground
black pepper
minced fresh chives

Wash potatoes and prick with a fork in several places. Bake for 60 to 70 minutes or until cooked. Turn oven to 325°F (160°C). Cut off the top third of each potato and scoop out insides leaving a ¼-inch (¾-cm) shell. Place cooked potato in bowl and mash until smooth. Add almost all the half-and-half plus the butter.

Using an electric mixer, beat until smooth, adding the remaining half-and-half, if necessary. Stir in ¾ of the cheese, and the bacon, salt, and pepper. Stuff the potato shells with the mixture, dividing evenly. Sprinkle with remaining cheese. Bake for 20 to 25 minutes or until cheese is melted and beginning to brown. Sprinkle with fresh chives.

In a large bowl, mix together potatoes, butter, Parmesan cheese, chives, basil, salt, and white pepper. Beat in egg yolks; fold in whipped cream. Beat egg whites until stiff and fold into potato mixture.

Spoon into 6 individual soufflé dishes or custard cups. Bake for 45 minutes or until golden brown.

INDIVIDUAL POTATO SOUFFLÉ

SERVES 6

Preheat oven to 350°F (180°C)

3 cups (340 g) cooked potatoes, put through ricer

¼ cup (60 g) butter, melted

¾ cup (85 g) grated Parmesan cheese

2 teaspoons minced fresh chives, or 1 teaspoon dried

½ teaspoon dried basil

1 teaspoon salt

½ teaspoon white pepper

3 eggs, separated

1 cup (240 mL) heavy cream, whipped

POTATOES ANNA

SERVES 6

Preheat oven to 450°F (230°C)

6 medium potatoes
½ cup (115 g) butter, melted
½ teaspoon salt

Peel potatoes and slice very thin, using a mandoline or a food processor. Brush an 8-inch (20-cm) round baking pan or a 9-inch (23-cm) pie plate with some of the butter. Beginning at the outer edge of the dish, begin arranging a circle of the potato slices in a neat pattern, overlapping them toward the center. Brush with some more melted butter and sprinkle with salt. Continue making layers until the potato slices and butter are used up.

Bake potatoes, uncovered, for 35 minutes. Then reduce heat to 350°F (180°C) and continue baking for 15 minutes more or until potatoes are tender. Run a knife around the edge of the pan and invert potatoes onto a serving plate. Cut in wedges to serve.

Wash potatoes, wipe dry, and rub with oil. Prick potatoes all over with fork. In a small bowl, mix chili powder, garlic powder, salt, pepper, cumin, and oregano. Roll potatoes in spice mixture and coat evenly. Wrap each potato in aluminum foil.

Roast in hot coals for about 1 hour or until potatoes are tender. Remove foil and slit potatoes in half. Place a piece of cheese on one half of each potato, cover with top halves, and rewrap with foil. Serve hot at once.

CAMPFIRE POTATOES

SERVES 4

Prepare coals for baking

4 large potatoes
1 tablespoon vegetable oil
2 teaspoons chili powder
2 teaspoons garlic powder
½ teaspoon salt
¼ teaspoon pepper
¼ teaspoon cumin
1½ teaspoons finely chopped fresh oregano, or ½ teaspoon dried
4 ounces (115 g) cheddar cheese, cut in 4 fingers

POTATO DUMPLINGS

MAKES ABOUT 16

3 medium potatoes
¼ cup (30 g) chopped onion
1 egg, beaten
½ cup (60 g) fresh bread crumbs
salt and pepper to taste
¼ cup (35 g) all-purpose flour,
approximately
croutons

Peel potatoes and cut in half. Cook the potatoes and onions in lightly salted water for 20 minutes or until tender. Drain, and put through a ricer or food mill.

Place the riced vegetables in a medium bowl and add the egg, bread crumbs, salt, and pepper to taste. Mix well. Stir in 3 tablespoons flour. If the dough is still sticky, add remaining flour. Gently roll into balls, about 1½ inches (4 cm) in diameter, adding a crouton in the center of each one. Gently drop potato balls into rapidly boiling water. Cook for about 8 minutes or until they rise to the surface and begin to look fluffy. Serve at once.

ETHNIC POTATOES

JANSSON'S TEMPTATION

SERVES 6

Preheat oven to 400°F (200°C)

1 can (2 ounces/60 g) flat anchovies
¼ cup (60 g) butter
2 cups (225 g) thinly sliced onions
6 medium potatoes, sliced thin
freshly ground pepper
2 cups (425 mL) half-and-half

Drain anchovies, reserving oil, and chop anchovies into small pieces. Melt 3 tablespoons (45 g) butter in a small skillet and sauté onions 5 minutes or until tender.

In a shallow 2-quart (2-L) baking pan, layer the potatoes, onions, and anchovies. Sprinkle with pepper and dot with remaining butter. Slowly pour in half-and-half until it covers the potatoes. Pour reserved anchovy oil over all. Cover. Bake for about 35 minutes. Remove cover and continue baking until potatoes are tender, about 15 minutes.

In a small skillet, melt 2 tablespoons (30 g) of the butter and sauté scallions for 3 minutes. Set aside. Cook potatoes in lightly salted water for 20 minutes or until tender. Drain, cool slightly, peel, and then mash.

In a small saucepan, heat the half-and-half with 2 tablespoons (30 g) of butter. Add to the mashed potatoes along with the scallions, salt, and white pepper. Place in baking pan. Make 6 indentations, and place 1 teaspoon of butter in each. Bake, uncovered, for about 10 minutes or until butter melts.

IRISH CHAMP

SERVES 6

Preheat oven to 400°F (200°C) and grease a shallow 2-quart (2-L) baking pan

6 tablespoons (90 g) butter
6 whole scallions, chopped
8 medium potatoes, peeled, cut in half
1½ cups (350 mL) half-and-half
salt and white pepper to taste

POTATO CURRY

SERVES 6

3 medium potatoes
1 eggplant, about 1 pound (450 g)
2 small, tender zucchini
2 tablespoons olive oil
1 teaspoon curry powder, or to taste
½ cup (125 mL) chicken broth
salt and pepper to taste
1 tomato, chopped
½ cup (125 mL) plain yogurt

Peel potatoes and cook for 15 minutes in slightly salted water. Drain and cut into ½-inch (1½-cm) dice.

Peel eggplant and zucchini, if desired. Cut into ½-inch (1½-cm) dice. Heat the oil and sauté the eggplant and zucchini for 2 minutes, stirring constantly. Add the potatoes and curry powder. Stir-fry for 2 minutes, then add the chicken broth and salt to taste. Cover and cook for 5 minutes over low heat or until vegetables are tender. Stir in tomato and yogurt and heat, but do not boil.

In a medium bowl, beat the eggs with a whisk until they are thick and light. Squeeze as much moisture as possible from the grated potatoes and add them to the eggs along with the flour, baking powder, salt and pepper, grated onion, and chicken fat. Mix well.

Spoon mixture into the casserole and bake for 1 hour or until golden brown.

POTATO KUGEL

SERVES 4 TO 6

Preheat oven to 350°F (180°C) and generously grease a 1-quart (1-L) casserole

3 eggs
3 cups (450 g) grated potatoes
⅓ cup (50 g) all-purpose flour
½ teaspoon baking powder
salt and pepper to taste
½ cup (75 g) grated onion
¼ cup (60 mL) rendered chicken fat
or butter, melted

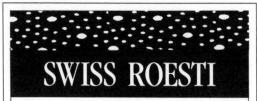

SWISS ROESTI

SERVES 4

4 medium russet potatoes
1 medium onion, finely minced
¼ cup (60 g) butter, approximately

In a large, heavy saucepan, cook potatoes in lightly salted water for 20 minutes or until tender. Drain and cool slightly. Peel and grate using large-hole side of a 4-sided grater. Add onion and mix well.

Melt 2 tablespoons (30 g) butter in a large heavy skillet. Spread potato mixture in pan and flatten with a spatula. Cook over medium heat for 10 minutes or until bottom is nicely browned. Shake pan occasionally so potatoes do not stick. Loosen around edges.

Place a dish on top and turn pan over.

Add remaining butter to pan and slide potato cake back and cook until other side is golden brown.

Soak the codfish in cold water for 4 to 6 hours, changing the water about every hour. Place fish in a medium saucepan and cover with water. Bring to a boil, taste water, and if it is still salty, drain and start with fresh water. Bring to a boil, lower heat, and simmer until fish is tender, about 10 to 15 minutes. Drain well and flake fish.

In a large, heavy saucepan, cook potatoes, covered, in lightly salted water for 20 minutes or until tender. Drain, cool slightly, and cut into quarters.

In a medium saucepan, heat olive oil and sauté onions and garlic 5 minutes or until onions are tender, taking care not to burn the onions. Add the flaked cod and the potatoes and stir lightly to combine. Turn onto a shallow serving dish and garnish with olives, salt and pepper, hard-cooked eggs, and parsley.

PORTUGUESE COD WITH POTATOES, ONIONS, & OLIVES

SERVES 4

1 pound (450 g) salted dry cod
4 medium potatoes, peeled
⅓ cup (75 mL) Spanish olive oil
2 onions, sliced
2 cloves garlic, smashed
½ cup (60 g) oil-cured olives
salt and pepper to taste
4 hard-cooked eggs, cut in wedges
chopped fresh Italian parsley
for garnish

SPANISH OMELET WITH POTATOES

SERVES 4

¼ cup (60 mL) olive oil
1 onion, sliced
1 green pepper, chopped
4 potatoes, cooked, peeled,
and sliced
¼ pound (115 g) cooked ham,
chopped
1 tomato, peeled, seeded,
and chopped
5 eggs
5 tablespoons (75 mL) milk
salt and pepper to taste
¼ pound (115 g) cheddar cheese,
shredded

In a large, heavy skillet, heat olive oil and sauté onion and green pepper 5 minutes or until tender. Stir in potato slices, ham, and tomato.

In a medium bowl, beat eggs and milk; season with salt and pepper. Pour eggs over vegetables in skillet and allow to set. Using a spatula, draw cooked egg away from side of pan and tilt pan to draw uncooked egg to edge. When eggs are almost set, spread with shredded cheddar cheese and run under broiler for a minute or so until cheese melts.

In a large saucepan, cook potatoes, covered, in lightly salted water for 20 minutes or until tender. Slice in half lengthwise and place on a broiler-proof serving dish cut side down. Lay the bacon slices over the potatoes and sprinkle with the chopped hard-cooked eggs. In a large, heavy skillet, heat olive oil and sauté onion for 5 minutes or until tender. Add tomatoes, chili peppers, chili powder, cumin, salt, and pepper. Cover; lower heat and simmer 10 minutes. Pour the sauce over the potatoes and cover with the cheese slices. Run under broiler for 2 minutes, or until cheese melts.

MEXICAN POTATOES

SERVES 6

6 potatoes, peeled
6 slices bacon, cooked and drained
4 hard-cooked eggs,
coarsely chopped
3 tablespoons olive oil
1 onion, chopped
2 cups (225 g) canned crushed
tomatoes
1 can (4 ounces/115 g) green chili
peppers, seeded and chopped
1 teaspoon chili powder
½ teaspoon cumin
salt and pepper to taste
¼ pound (115 g) Monterey jack
cheese, sliced

POTATO GNOCCHI WITH TOMATO SAUCE

SERVES 4

4 potatoes, peeled and cut into chunks
¾ cup (100 g) all-purpose flour
1 egg
salt and freshly ground pepper to taste
1 tablespoon olive oil
1 slice prosciutto, chopped
1 clove garlic, smashed
1 onion, chopped
2 cups (225 g) canned crushed tomatoes
1 tablespoon finely chopped fresh basil, or 1 teaspoon dried
salt and pepper to taste
Parmesan cheese

In a large, heavy saucepan, cook potatoes, covered, in lightly salted water 20 minutes or until tender. Drain well and mash. Add flour, egg, salt, and pepper. Mix until dough holds together. Roll out on a well-floured surface into a rope about ½ inch (1½ cm) thick. Cut into 1-inch (2½-cm) lengths. Dry slightly.

Drop gnocchi into 4 quarts (4 L) of boiling, lightly salted water. Cook for about 5 minutes or until tender. Drain well.

To make sauce, heat olive oil in a large saucepan; sauté prosciutto, garlic, and onion for 5 minutes or until onion is tender. Add tomatoes and basil, salt, and pepper. Simmer for 15 minutes. Pour sauce over gnocchi and sprinkle liberally with Parmesan cheese.

Opposite: Potatoes with Green Beans & Red Onions (p. 38)

In a medium skillet, heat 3 tablespoons (45 mL) olive oil. Fry potatoes over medium heat for 10 minutes or until tender. Drain on paper towels and place in a shallow serving dish.

Add remaining 3 tablespoons (45 mL) olive oil to skillet and heat. Sauté garlic, green and red peppers, and onion for 5 minutes or until tender. Add tomato, olives, orange peel, basil, wine, salt, and pepper. Cook for 3 minutes, stirring constantly. Remove orange peel. Spoon vegetables around potatoes and garnish with chopped parsley.

POTATOES PROVENÇALE

SERVES 6

6 tablespoons (90 mL) olive oil
4 potatoes, peeled and sliced
2 cloves garlic, smashed
1 small green pepper, cut into strips
1 small red pepper, cut into strips
2 medium onions, cut in rings
3 ripe tomatoes, peeled, seeded, and chopped
⅓ cup (35 g) pitted ripe olives, halved
1 strip fresh orange peel
1 tablespoon finely chopped fresh basil, or 1 teaspoon dried
½ cup (125 mL) dry white wine
salt and pepper to taste
chopped fresh Italian parsley for garnish

POTATO MAIN DISHES

POTATO PIE

SERVES 8

Preheat oven to 400°F (200°C)

4 medium potatoes, peeled
2 tablespoons (30 g) butter
2 tablespoons heavy cream
1 container (15 ounces/425 g)
ricotta cheese
1 cup (240 mL) sour cream
½ cup (60 g) grated Parmesan cheese
2 eggs, slightly beaten
1 teaspoon salt
½ teaspoon freshly ground
black pepper
¼ teaspoon grated nutmeg
6 scallions, chopped
1 unbaked 10-inch (25-cm) pie shell

In a large, heavy saucepan, cook potatoes in lightly salted water for 20 minutes or until tender. Drain potatoes and mash until smooth. Place in a medium bowl and beat in butter and cream.

Add ricotta, sour cream, Parmesan cheese, eggs, salt, pepper, nutmeg, and scallions, blending well. Pour into unbaked pie shell. Bake for 50 to 60 minutes or until golden.

In a large skillet, heat oil and sauté onion and garlic for 5 minutes or until onion is tender. Stir in salt, pepper, basil, and oregano. Add tomatoes and mix well.

Arrange potato slices in a well-greased, shallow 1-quart (1-L) baking dish. Spoon tomatoes over potatoes and sprinkle with Parmesan cheese. Cover dish with aluminum foil. Bake for 30 minutes. Remove foil and cook, uncovered, for about 10 minutes or until potatoes are tender. Remove dish from oven and sprinkle with mozarella cheese. Run dish under broiler until cheese melts, about 2 minutes.

SCALLOPED POTATOES AND TOMATOES WITH CHEESE

SERVES 4

Preheat oven to 400°F (200°C)

2 tablespoons olive oil
1 onion, coarsely chopped
2 cloves garlic
salt and pepper to taste
1½ teaspoons finely chopped fresh basil, or ½ teaspoon dried
1½ teaspoons finely chopped fresh oregano, or ½ teaspoon dried
2 large ripe tomatoes, peeled, seeded, and chopped
2 cups (225 g) thinly sliced peeled potatoes
¼ cup (30 g) grated Parmesan cheese
½ cup (60 g) shredded mozzarella cheese

LITTLE SHEPHERD'S PIES

SERVES 4

Preheat oven to 475°F (240°C)

1 tablespoon vegetable oil
1 small onion, chopped
½ green pepper, chopped
2 cups (450 g) chopped
  leftover lamb or beef
salt and pepper to taste
4 large russet potatoes, baked
2 tablespoons heavy cream
4 ounces (115 g) cheddar cheese,
  shredded
2 tablespoons (30 g) butter, melted

In a large skillet, heat the oil and sauté the onion and green pepper for 5 minutes. Add the meat and stir fry until hot, about 1 minute. Season to taste with salt and pepper.

Cut the potatoes in half lengthwise and scoop out the pulp, leaving a ¼-inch (¾-cm) shell. Place potato pulp in a small bowl and mash well. Mix in the cream, cheese, meat mixture, salt, and pepper.

Spoon the mixture into the potato shells, mounding the tops. Drizzle each with butter, then place shells in a shallow pan and bake for about 15 minutes, or until lightly browned.

In a large saucepan, cover potatoes with lightly salted water and cook for 20 minutes or until tender. Drain, peel, and slice potatoes. In a large skillet, melt butter and sauté scallions, paprika, and mushrooms 2 minutes.

In a shallow, greased 2-quart (2-L) baking dish, layer half the potatoes, mushroom mixture, and cheese. Repeat. In a large bowl, beat eggs, milk, salt, pepper, and tarragon. Pour over vegetables in baking dish. Bake for 50 to 60 minutes or until custard is set. Cover with sliced tomatoes and return to oven 5 minutes.

POTATO MUSHROOM CHEESE BAKE

SERVES 4

Preheat oven to 325°F (160°C)

4 potatoes
2 tablespoons (30 g) butter
¼ cup (7 g) chopped scallions
¼ teaspoon paprika
½ pound (225 g) mushrooms, sliced
½ pound (225 g) cheddar cheese, shredded
4 eggs
2 cups (425 mL) milk
salt and pepper to taste
1½ teaspoons finely chopped fresh tarragon, or ½ teaspoon dried
2 tomatoes, sliced

POTATO PASTITSIO

SERVES 6

Preheat oven to 350°F (180°C) and grease an 8-inch (20-cm) square baking dish

4 russet potatoes
2 tablespoons olive oil
1 pound (450 g) lean ground round or lamb
1 cup (114 g) chopped onions
½ cup (125 mL) tomato sauce
2 tablespoons dry white wine
salt and pepper to taste
2 eggs
½ cup (60 g) crumbled feta cheese
½ cup (60 mL) milk
½ cup (60 g) bread crumbs
2 tablespoons (30 g) butter

Cook the potatoes in lightly salted water about 20 minutes or until tender. Drain, cool slightly, peel, and cut lengthwise into ¼-inch (¾-cm) slices.

In a large skillet, heat 1 tablespoon of the oil and cook the meat and onions until meat is brown. Add the tomato sauce, wine, salt, and pepper. Simmer for 15 minutes.

Make a layer of half the potato slices in the baking dish. Cover with half the sauce. Repeat. Combine the eggs, cheese, and milk in a bowl, then pour over all. Sprinkle with bread crumbs and dot with butter. Bake, uncovered, for 30 minutes. Allow to sit 15 minutes before serving.

Opposite: Baked Potato with sour cream & salmon caviar (p. 74)

In a medium bowl, mix together ground beef, onion, green pepper, parsley, tomato, Tabasco, salt, and pepper. Pat half the mixture into the bottom of a greased 10-inch (25-cm) pie pan.

Peel potatoes and slice thin. Arrange the potato slices over meat mixture, overlapping slices. Sprinkle with half the cheddar cheese. Pat the remaining meat mixture on top. Cover with aluminum foil.

Bake for 45 minutes. Remove foil and pour off any fat from meat. Sprinkle with remaining cheese and return dish to oven for an additional 20 minutes or until potatoes are tender.

MEAT AND POTATO PIE

SERVES 4 TO 6
Preheat oven to 350°F (180°C)

¾ pound (340 g) lean ground beef
1 small onion, chopped
½ green pepper, chopped
2 tablespoons chopped fresh
Italian parsley
1 small tomato, peeled, seeded,
and chopped
¼ teaspoon Tabasco sauce
1 teaspoon salt
¼ teaspoon pepper
4 medium potatoes
1 cup (115 g) shredded
cheddar cheese

RANGER POTATO HASH

SERVES 4

4 medium potatoes
2 cups (450 g) chunked leftover roasted meat (beef or lamb)
1 large onion, minced
1 teaspoon salt
½ teaspoon pepper
2 tablespoons (30 g) butter
2 tablespoons vegetable oil
4 eggs, fried as desired

Peel potatoes and then grate, using the large-hole side of a 4-sided grater or the grating blade of a food processor. Chop the meat fine or use a food processor.

Combine the potatoes, meat, onion, salt, and pepper in a bowl. Mix well.

In a large, heavy skillet, melt the butter and heat with the oil. Place the potato mixture in the pan, press down with a spatula, and fry until brown and crusty on the bottom, shaking the pan frequently to prevent burning.

Remove pan from heat. Place a dinner plate on top and, holding both together, turn upside down. Slide the hash off the plate and back into the pan. Add additional butter and oil, if necessary, and cook until the potatoes are tender.

Divide hash into 4 sections and place on individual plates. Top each with a fried egg and serve at once.

Cut the eggplants into ½-inch (1½-cm) cubes. Sprinkle with salt, place in a colander, put a weight on top, and allow to drain for 1 hour. Rinse, drain, and pat dry with paper towels.

Cut the lamb into steaks and season with salt and pepper. In a large roasting pan, heat the olive oil and brown the garlic. Add the lamb steaks and quickly sear on both sides over high heat.

Place the steaks in a single layer in the pan and sprinkle with chopped bacon. Make 2 layers of potatoes, eggplant, thyme, and rosemary, then place the pan in the oven and bake, uncovered, for 30 minutes.

Remove pan and cover tightly with a lid or with a double thickness of aluminum foil. Reduce the oven heat to 350°F (180°C) and bake an additional 2 hours or until the meat and vegetables are tender.

LAMB WITH POTATOES AND EGGPLANT

SERVES 8

Preheat the oven to 450°F (230°C)

2 eggplants, 1 pound (450 g) each
salt
1 leg of lamb, about 4 pounds (1¾ kg), boned and rolled
freshly ground pepper
2 tablespoons olive oil
2 cloves garlic, smashed
4 slices bacon, chopped
6 medium potatoes, peeled and sliced ¼-inch thick
1 teaspoon dried thyme
1 teaspoon dried rosemary

HUNGARIAN PORK CUTLETS WITH POTATOES

SERVES 6

Preheat the oven to 350°F (180°C) and grease a shallow 2-quart (2-L) baking dish

4 medium potatoes
1 pound (450 g) pork cutlets, cut thin
salt and pepper to taste
flour for dredging
3 tablespoons vegetable oil
1 cup (115 g) sliced onions
2 cloves garlic, smashed
1 large green pepper,
cut into squares
½ cup (125 mL) chicken broth
1 teaspoon Hungarian paprika
¼ teaspoon caraway seeds
2 tomatoes, peeled, seeded,
and cut into chunks

Peel the potatoes and cut into ¼-inch (¾-cm) slices. Cook in lightly salted water for 10 minutes. Drain well.

Dredge the pork cutlets in flour seasoned with salt and pepper. Heat 2 tablespoons of the oil in a large skillet and brown the cutlets on both sides.

Place the potatoes in the baking dish and put the pork cutlets on top. In the same skillet that you cooked the cutlets, heat the remaining oil and stir-fry the onions, garlic, and green pepper for 5 minutes, taking care not to burn them.

Layer the onion mixture over the cutlets. Pour the chicken broth into the skillet and bring to a boil. Loosen the particles stuck to the pan, then stir in the paprika, salt to taste, and caraway seeds. Pour over the cutlets. Cover tightly, and bake in oven for 20 to 25 minutes, or until the potatoes are tender.

Remove the cover and add the tomato chunks. Return dish to oven, uncovered, and bake until tomatoes are hot, about 10 minutes.

POTATO SNACKS

BAKED POTATO SKINS

SERVES 6

Preheat oven to 400°F (200°C)

6 potatoes
¼ cup (60 g) butter, melted
coarse salt

Scrub potatoes and pat dry. Pierce in several places with fork. Bake potatoes about 45 to 60 minutes or until tender. Cool slightly and then cut in half. Scoop out flesh leaving ⅛- to ¼-inch (½- to ¾-cm) shell. (Reserve flesh for recipes calling for mashed or riced potatoes.) Turn oven up to 500°F (260°C).

Using a kitchen shears, cut the shells in half and then in half again, giving you 8 sections for each potato. Brush both sides of skins with melted butter and sprinkle with coarse salt. Place on a baking sheet. Bake about 10 to 12 minutes or until crisp.

Scrub potatoes and pat dry. Pierce in several places with a fork. Bake potatoes about 45 to 60 minutes or until tender. Cool slightly and then cut in half. Scoop out flesh, leaving 1/8- to 1/4-inch (1/2- to 3/4-cm) shell. (Reserve flesh for recipes calling for mashed or riced potatoes.)

Using a kitchen shears, cut the shells in half and then in half again, giving you 8 sections for each potato. Heat vegetable oil in deep-fat fryer to 360°F (180°C) and fry skins until they are crisp. Drain well and sprinkle with salt.

FRIED POTATO SKINS

SERVES 6
Preheat oven to 400°F (200°C)

6 potatoes
vegetable oil for deep-frying
coarse salt

Suggested Toppings

These toppings require no additional cooking.

shredded cheddar cheese and
 crumbled bacon (just run under the
 broiler)
sour cream and chives
shredded Swiss cheese
cottage cheese
smoked salmon
tuna fish salad
egg salad

71

HOT SALSA DIP FOR POTATO SKINS

MAKES ABOUT 3 CUPS

2 cups (225 g) peeled, seeded, and chopped fresh tomatoes

1 can (4 ounces/225 g) green chilies, seeded and chopped

1 small onion, minced

¼ cup (30 g) chopped green pepper

1 jalapeño chili pepper, canned or fresh, seeded and chopped

2 tablespoons fresh cilantro

salt and pepper to taste

In a small bowl, combine tomatoes, chilies, onion, green pepper, jalapeño, cilantro, salt, and pepper.

Opposite: Fried Potato Skins with a Garlic Dip (pp. 71, 73)

In a small bowl, combine the garlic, mustard, and egg yolks and stir until well blended. Combine the vegetable and olive oils and slowly add the oils, a drop at a time at first, beating constantly. As the mixture begins to thicken, add oil a little faster and beat until the mixture is smooth. Add the lemon juice, salt, and pepper.

GARLIC DIP FOR POTATO SKINS

MAKES ABOUT 1¼ CUPS

6 cloves garlic, finely minced
4 teaspoons Dijon-style mustard
2 egg yolks, slightly beaten
½ cup (125 mL) vegetable oil
½ cup (125 mL) olive oil
1 tablespoon lemon juice
salt and pepper to taste

BAKED POTATOES

SERVES 6

Preheat oven to 400°F (200°C)

6 russet potatoes

Wash potatoes and pat dry. Prick in several places with a fork or make ½-inch (1½-cm) slits with a sharp paring knife on 2 sides. Bake potatoes for about 1 hour. Test for doneness by squeezing gently with a towel or inserting a sharp paring knife in the center.

Suggested Toppings (require little or no cooking)

Nothing tastes better on a freshly baked potato than a pat of butter and salt and freshly ground black pepper. Here are a few other easy suggestions:

sour cream and caviar
creamy salad dressing
yogurt with chives
poached egg
pesto sauce
crumbled blue cheese
shredded cheddar cheese

In a medium saucepan, heat 1 tablespoon oil and cook beef until brown, breaking up any lumps. Remove from pan.

In same saucepan, heat remaining 1 tablespoon oil and sauté onion, green pepper, celery and garlic for 5 minutes or until vegetables are tender. Add beef, chili powder, cumin, tomatoes, salt, and pepper and cook for 20 minutes. Spoon over baked potatoes. Top with avocado slices, if you wish.

CHILI TOPPING FOR BAKED POTATO

MAKES TOPPING FOR 6 POTATOES

2 tablespoons vegetable oil
½ pound (225 g) ground beef
1 small onion, chopped
½ green pepper, chopped
1 stalk celery, chopped
1 clove garlic, crushed
1 tablespoon chili powder
(or to taste)
½ teaspoon cumin
2 cups (225 g) crushed, peeled, and seeded tomatoes
salt and pepper to taste
sliced avocado (optional)

VEGETABLE CHEESE TOPPING FOR BAKED POTATO

MAKES TOPPING FOR 6 POTATOES

2 tablespoons (30 g) butter
½ cup (60 g) chopped green pepper
1 small onion, chopped
1 can (8 ounces/225 g) cream-style corn
1 tomato, peeled, seeded and chopped
½ medium zucchini, diced
salt and pepper to taste
¾ teaspoon finely chopped fresh oregano, or ¼ teaspoon dried
½ cup (60 g) shredded Monterey jack cheese
2 tablespoons grated Parmesan cheese

In a medium skillet, heat butter and sauté pepper and onion 5 minutes or until tender. Add corn, tomato, zucchini, salt, pepper, and oregano. Cook for 5 minutes. Stir in Monterey jack cheese. Cover and heat thoroughly, but do not boil.

Split potatoes open and spoon vegetables on top. Sprinkle with Parmesan cheese.

Cook frozen broccoli according to package directions. If using fresh broccoli, pare stems and place stalks and flowerettes in steamer basket. Lower into saucepan containing 1 inch (2½ cm) salted boiling water and steam 15 minutes or until crisp-tender.

In a medium saucepan, melt butter and stir in flour, salt and pepper to make a smooth paste. Cook for 1 minute off heat. Return to stove and gradually add half-and-half, beating vigorously. Cook and stir until mixture thickens and then simmer 2 minutes.

Add shredded cheddar cheese off the heat and stir until melted. Pour cheese sauce over broccoli in medium bowl and stir gently to cover. Split potatoes open and spoon sauce on top.

BROCCOLI AND CHEESE TOPPING FOR BAKED POTATO

MAKES TOPPING FOR 6 POTATOES

1 package (10 ounces/285 g) frozen broccoli spears, or 1 small bunch fresh broccoli

3 tablespoons (45 g) butter

2 tablespoons all-purpose flour

salt and pepper to taste

1½ cups (350 mL) half-and-half

1 cup (115 g) shredded cheddar cheese

SEAFOOD TOPPING FOR BAKED POTATO

MAKES TOPPING FOR 6 POTATOES

3 tablespoons (45 g) butter
2 tablespoons all-purpose flour
salt and pepper to taste
½ cup (225 g) chopped mushrooms
1½ cups (350 mL) half-and-half
½ cup (85 g) chopped cooked shrimp
½ cup (85 g) flaked crab meat

In a medium saucepan, melt butter and stir in flour, salt, and pepper to make a smooth paste. Cook 1 minute off heat. Add mushrooms. Return to stove and gradually add half-and-half, stirring vigorously. Cook until mixture thickens and then simmer 2 minutes.

Add shrimp and crab meat and heat thoroughly but do not boil. Split potatoes open and spoon sauce over top.

POTATO CREPES

POTATO CREPES

MAKES 12 CREPES

2 cups (225 g) unseasoned
mashed potatoes
2 tablespoons light cream
1 tablespoon butter, melted
salt and pepper to taste
1 cup (140 g) all-purpose flour
(approximately)
vegetable oil

In a large bowl, mix the mashed potatoes, cream, butter, salt, and pepper. Add ¾ cup (100 g) flour and mix well. Turn out on a lightly floured surface and knead briefly, adding additional flour as needed.

Divide into 12 equal-size balls and roll each into a 7-inch (18-cm) circle on a lightly floured surface. Cover surface of a heavy skillet or crepe pan with oil and heat. Cook crepes, one at a time, about 1 minute on each side or until lightly browned.

Opposite: Potato Crepes with Apple Cranberry Filling

In a medium saucepan, combine apple slices, orange peel, apple juice, sugar, and butter. Cook over medium heat, stirring occasionally, about 10 minutes or until apples are crisp-tender. Stir in whole cranberry sauce and nuts. Cook for 5 minutes longer over medium heat.

Place potato crepes on individual dishes. Spoon about 1/3 cup (75 mL) apple mixture down center of each crepe. Fold over sides to enclose filling. Spoon pan juices over crepes. Top with whipped cream and dust with cinnamon.

APPLE CRANBERRY FILLING FOR POTATO CREPES

SERVES 6

3 thinly sliced, peeled Granny Smith apples
2 teaspoons freshly grated orange peel
¼ cup (60 mL) apple juice
¼ cup (40 g) brown sugar
2 tablespoons (30 g) butter
1 can (8 ounces/225 g) whole cranberry sauce
¼ cup (30 g) chopped walnuts
6 Potato Crepes (page 80)
lightly sweetened whipped cream
ground cinnamon

TURKEY FILLING FOR POTATO CREPES

SERVES 6

Preheat oven to 375°F (190°C)

2 tablespoons (30 g) butter
½ cup (60 g) chopped celery
3 scallions, sliced
1 teaspoon dry mustard
2 tablespoons all-purpose flour
1½ cups (350 mL) half-and-half
¼ teaspoon salt
⅛ teaspoon pepper
¾ teaspoon finely chopped fresh thyme, or ¼ teaspoon dried
1 cup (115 g) sliced mushrooms
¼ cup (30 g) cooked green peas
2 cups (340 g) diced cooked turkey
6 Potato Crepes (page 80)
shredded cheddar cheese

In a large saucepan, melt butter. Add celery, scallions, and mustard; cook for 3 minutes or until vegetables are tender. Stir in flour and cook for 1 minute off the heat. Return to heat and gradually add half-and-half, stirring constantly with a whisk until mixture thickens, about 5 minutes. Add salt, pepper, thyme, mushrooms, peas and turkey. Cook for 5 minutes, stirring occasionally.

Spoon about ½ cup (125 mL) hot turkey mixture down center of each crepe. Lap sides over center and place in ovenproof dish. Sprinkle with cheddar cheese. Bake for 15 minutes or until cheese melts.

POTATO BAKED GOODS

POTATO PIZZA

SERVES 8

Preheat oven to 450°F (230°C)

1 cup (175 g) unseasoned
mashed potatoes
1 cup (240 mL) water from cooking
potatoes, 105 to 110°F (40 to 43°C)
1 tablespoon granulated sugar
1 envelope (7 g) active dry yeast
1 teaspoon salt
½ cup (125 mL) olive oil
4 to 4½ cups (560 to 630 g)
all-purpose flour
2 cloves garlic, finely chopped
⅔ cup (85 g) grated Parmesan cheese
1 tablespoon finely chopped fresh
oregano, or 1 teaspoon dried
1 tablespoon finely chopped fresh
basil, or 1 teaspoon dried
6 scallions, chopped
2 tablespoons olive oil
1 red pepper, halved, seeded
and chopped
1 large onion, chopped
2 ounces (60 g) prosciutto, chopped

In a large mixing bowl, combine potatoes, potato liquid, sugar, and yeast. Stir slightly and allow to rest at room temperature for 20 minutes.

Stir in salt and ¼ cup (60 mL) olive oil. Add 4 cups (560 g) flour, 1 cup (140 g) at a time, stirring to combine well after each addition. Turn dough out on a lightly floured surface and knead until smooth, using additional ½ cup (70 g) flour, if necessary. Place dough in a greased bowl, grease the top, and cover with plastic wrap. Set in a warm place and allow to rise for about 1 hour.

Punch dough down in bowl and leave it there for 15 minutes. Turn dough out onto a lightly floured surface and roll into a 10 × 15-inch (25 × 38-cm) rectangle. Place in a greased jelly roll pan. Brush surface with ¼ cup (60 mL) olive oil and sprinkle with garlic, Parmesan cheese, oregano, basil, and scallions. Heat 2 tablespoons olive oil in a medium skillet and sauté red pepper and onion 3 minutes. Arrange vegetables over top of dough and sprinkle with chopped prosciutto. Set aside to rise, uncovered, for 30 minutes. Bake for about 15 minutes or until edges are brown and crispy.

In a large mixing bowl, sprinkle yeast over potato water and stir until dissolved. Stir in potatoes, honey, milk, butter, salt, and 3 cups (420 g) flour with a wooden spoon. Beat until smooth. Add 7 cups (1 kg) flour, 1 cup (140 g) at a time, beating well after each addition. Turn out onto floured surface and knead until smooth, about 10 minutes. Use additional ½ cup (70 g) flour, if necessary. Dough will be slightly sticky. Place dough in a greased bowl, grease top of dough and cover with plastic wrap. Allow to rise for 1 hour.

Punch down and divide into 3 balls. Roll each out to a 9-inch (23-cm) square and roll up tightly. Place each in a greased 9 × 5 × 3-inch (23 × 13 × 7½-cm) loaf pan. Grease 3 pieces of plastic wrap and cover each loaf. Allow to rise about 45 minutes or until dough reaches the top of the pan.

Bake about 35 minutes. Remove loaves from pans and return to oven for 5 minutes longer.

POTATO BREAD

MAKES 3 LOAVES
Preheat oven to 350°F (180°C)

2 envelopes (7 g each) active dry yeast
1 cup (240 mL) water from cooking potatoes, between 105°-115°F (40°-46°C)
1 cup (175 g) unseasoned mashed potatoes
2 tablespoons honey
2 cups (425 mL) milk
3 tablespoons (45 g) butter, softened
2 teaspoons salt
7 to 7½ cups (900 g) all-purpose flour

POTATO KNISHES

MAKES 24 KNISHES

Preheat oven to 400°F (200°C)

3 cups (420 g) all-purpose flour
1 teaspoon salt
¾ teaspoon baking powder
½ cup (115 g) solid white vegetable shortening
½ cup (125 mL) water from cooking potatoes
4 pounds (1¾ kg) potatoes
½ cup (125 mL) butter (or chicken fat)
2 large onions, chopped
2 cloves garlic, minced
3 eggs, slightly beaten
1 teaspoon salt
¼ teaspoon white pepper
1 egg beaten with 1 tablespoon milk for glaze

In a large bowl, combine flour, salt, and baking powder. Cut in shortening using pastry blender, 2 knives, or your fingertips. With a fork, stir in potato water and work dough until it forms a smooth ball. Divide into fourths and roll each one out on a lightly floured surface into a 12 × 8-inch (30 × 20-cm) rectangle.

Peel potatoes and cook them in lightly salted water 20 minutes or until tender. Drain well and put through ricer.

In a medium skillet, heat butter and sauté onions and garlic 5 minutes or until tender. Add to potatoes with eggs, salt, and pepper and mix well. There should be 6 cups (1400 mL) filling.

Spoon 1½ cups (350 mL) filling down center third of each rectangle of dough. Fold sides over very loosely and turn rolls over onto a greased baking sheet. Slash each roll crosswise at 2-inch (5-cm) intervals using a serrated knife. Brush with egg glaze. Bake for 45 minutes. When cool cut through slashes.

POTATO DESSERTS

CHOCOLATE POTATO CAKE

SERVES 12

Preheat oven to 350°F (180°C)

1 cup (225 g) butter
2 cups (380 g) granulated sugar
4 eggs
3 ounces (85 g) unsweetened
chocolate, melted
½ cup (85 g) cold unseasoned
mashed potatoes
1 teaspoon ground cinnamon
1 teaspoon grated fresh orange peel
¼ teaspoon grated nutmeg
2 cups (280 g) all-purpose flour
1 teaspoon baking soda
1 cup (240 mL) milk
1 tablespoon lemon juice
1 cup (115 g) coarsely chopped
filberts (hazelnuts)
cocoa for dusting pan
whipped cream and chopped filberts
(hazelnuts) for garnish

In a large bowl, cream butter and sugar with electric mixer at high speed. Add eggs, 1 at a time, beating well after each addition. Add melted chocolate, mashed potatoes, cinnamon, orange peel, and nutmeg.

Combine flour and baking soda. Combine milk and lemon juice. Add flour to chocolate mixture alternately with milk beginning and ending with dry ingredients. Stir in chopped filberts. Grease a 9-inch (23-cm) spring-form pan and dust with cocoa. Spoon batter into pan. Bake for 1 hour and 30 minutes or until a cake tester inserted in center of cake comes out clean. Cool in pan 20 minutes.

Remove side; cool cake completely. Garnish with whipped cream and sprinkle with chopped filberts.

In a large bowl, beat eggs with an electric mixer until light and lemon colored. While still beating, add sugar gradually and beat until sugar is dissolved. Add cocoa, butter, and mashed potatoes to egg mixture. Combine vinegar with milk and add to mixture. Mix well.

Combine flour, baking powder, baking soda, salt, and mace. Add to bowl and mix well. Turn onto a floured surface and roll to 1/2-inch (1 1/2-cm) thickness. Cut with a doughnut cutter, rerolling scraps.

Heat vegetable oil to 365°F (190°C) in deep-fat fryer or large saucepan. Fry 1 minute or until golden. Turn and fry until done. Drain on paper toweling. Dust with confectioners sugar.

CHOCOLATE POTATO DOUGHNUTS

MAKES ABOUT 30 DOUGHNUTS

3 eggs
1 cup (190 g) firmly packed brown sugar
1/2 cup (70 g) cocoa powder
1/2 cup (115 g) butter, softened
1 cup (175 g) unseasoned mashed potatoes
1 teaspoon white distilled vinegar
1 cup (240 mL) milk
5 cups (700 g) all-purpose flour
4 teaspoons baking powder
1 teaspoon baking soda
1 teaspoon salt
1/4 teaspoon mace
vegetable oil
confectioners sugar

INDEX

Anna, Potatoes, 44

Baked Potatoes, 74; Toppings for, 75–78; Twice-Baked, 42
Baked Potato Skins, 70
Beef: Little Shepherd's Pies, 62; Meat and Potato Pie, 65; Potato Pastitsio, 64; and Potato Soup, Hungarian Style, 28; Ranger Potato Hash, 66
Bread, Potato, 85

Cake, Chocolate Potato, 88
California Potato Salad, 31
Campfire Potatoes, 45
Carrots and New Potatoes, 34
Chicken and Potato Salad, Curried, 29
Chips, Potato, 15
Chocolate: Potato Cake, 88; Potato Doughnuts, 89
Cod (Portuguese) with Potatoes, Onions, and Olives, 53
Cream of Potato Soup, 25
Crepes, Potato, 80; Fillings for, 81–82
Curried Chicken and Potato Salad, 29
Curry, Potato, 50

Desserts, 88–89
Dips: Garlic, 73; Hot Salsa, 72
Doughnuts, Chocolate Potato, 89
Dumplings, Potato, 46

Eggplant and Potatoes, Lamb with, 67

French-Fried Potatoes, 14
Fried Potatoes and Onions, 18
Fried Potato Skins, 71
Fritters: Potato, 40; Potato-Zucchini, 39

Gnocchi (Potato) with Tomato Sauce, 56
Green Beans and Red Onions, Potatoes with, 38

Ham-and-Eggs Potato Salad, Hot, 30
Hash Brown Potatoes, 16
Hash, Ranger Potato, 66

Irish Champ, 49

Jansson's Temptation, 48

Knishes, Potato, 86
Kugel, Potato, 51

Lamb: Little Shepherd's Pies, 62; Potato Pastitsio, 64; Potatoes and Eggplant with, 67; Ranger Potato Hash, 66

Mashed Potatoes, 22; and Rutabagas, 35
Meat and Potato Pie, 65
Mexican Potatoes, 55
Mushroom Cheese Bake, Potato, 63
Mussel Potato Chowder, 26

New Potatoes: and Carrots, 34; with Parsley and Butter, 19

Omelet (Spanish) with Potatoes, 54
Oven-Fried Potato Wedges, 17

Pancakes, Potato, 21
Pastitsio, Potato, 64
Peppers, Potato-Stuffed, 37
Pie, Potato, 60
Pizza, Potato, 84
Polish Potato and Sausage Soup, 24
Pork Cutlets, Hungarian, with Potatoes, 68
Provençale, Potatoes, 57

Ranger Potato Hash, 66
Red Onions and Green Beans, Potatoes with, 38
Roasted Potatoes, 20
Roesti, Swiss, 52
Rutabagas and Mashed Potatoes, 35

Salads, 29–32
Sausage and Potato Soup, Polish, 24
Scalloped Potatoes, with Tomatoes and
    Cheese, 61
Shepherd's Pies, Little, 62
Skins, Potato: Baked, 70; Dips for, 72–73;
    Fried, 71
Soufflé, Individual Potato, 43
Soups, 24–28
Spinach and Potato Casserole, 36
Stuffing (Potato) for Turkey, 41
Swiss Roesti, 52

Toppings (for Baked Potatoes): Broccoli and
    Cheese, 77; Chili, 75; Seafood, 78; Vegetable
    Cheese, 76
Turkey Potato Chowder, 27

Vegetable Potato Salad, 32

Zucchini-Potato Fritters, 39

FAVORITE RECIPES

FAVORITE RECIPES

_____

_____

_____

_____

_____

_____

_____

_____

_____

_____

_____

_____

FAVORITE RECIPES

FAVORITE RECIPES

Marie Bianco is a food writer for Long Island's newspaper Newsday. *She is the author of two other Barron's books,* 32 Seafood Dishes *and* 32 Fabulous Cookies.